~ LINES FOR ALL OCCASIONS ~

Clichés & Platitudes

KNOCK KNOCK®

VENICE, CALIFORNIA

Children should be seen and not heard.

———•·•———

Spare the rod and spoil the child.

———•·•———

A child may have too much
of his mother's blessing.

———•·•———

A bustling mother makes
a slothful daughter.

———•·•———

An indulgent mother makes
a sluttish daughter.

———•·•———

A son's a son until he takes a wife, but
a daughter's a daughter all her life.

———•·•———

Parents can give us everything
but common sense.

———•·•———

The hand that rocks the cradle is
the hand that rules the world.

Just wait until you have kids.

———◆———

Parents who are afraid to put
their foot down usually have
children who step on their toes.

———◆———

For the good stepmother there
is a golden chair in heaven.

———◆———

Honor thy father and thy mother.

———◆———

Do as I say, not as I do.

———◆———

Because I said so.

Community

Good fences make good neighbors.

———◆———

Everyone is nice until the
cow gets into the garden.

Love thy neighbor as thyself.

———•·•———

Think globally, act locally.

———•·•———

Each person's homeland is dear to him.

———•·•———

There's safety in numbers.

———•·•———

It takes a village to raise a child.

No, YOU Have a Nice Day

So ubiquitous as to be unconscious, "Have a nice day" is a reflexive, essentially meaningless salutation. This platitude became common in American trucker vernacular in the 1950s. Then, with late 1960s mass-market irony, it was used as a snarky rejoinder to an unpleasant encounter. As such, in 1988, the Brunswick, Maine, police chief ordered officers to stop using the phrase, particularly after issuing moving violations.

Choose the neighbor before the house.

If everyone swept in front of his house,
the whole town would be clean.

Thou shalt not covet thy neighbor's wife.

In a village, do as the village does.

Hawks will not pick out hawks' eyes.

A public insult requires a public apology.

Every sandpiper praises his own swamp.

Birds of a feather flock together.

Live and let live.

Do as others do, and few will mock you.

He that is unkind to his own
will not be kind to others.

A community is as those who rule it.

Become not a priest in your hometown,
nor marry far away from it.

Close neighbors are better
than distant relatives.

United we stand, divided we fall.

Live together or die alone.

---

up
tion,
the lan-
ugh Proverbs
life, culture,
gion, and history."

H. Auden said, "Some
undeservedly forgotten;
e undeservedly remem-
. The Canadian *National Post*
ted, "Possibly that rule applies
also to words, terms, phrases, even
comparisons to icebergs. Longevity
confirms their value." Art, ideas,
performances, and gastronomy last
in our collective memories just as

Lost in Translation

When it comes to international relations, language matters; a misinterpreted idiomatic phrase could spark global conflict. Fortunately the powers that be recognize this. During the Cold War, President Richard Nixon studied on Russian maxims to facilitate negotia and today the United Nations offer guage course Arabic Culture Th "to investigate the patterns of politics, ethics, society, reli

The poet W
books are
none ar
bered
n

cur
platform from w
and dissect the makeup of
tion itself.

clichés endure, so it is only fitting that we apply these time-tested words to our cultural endeavors.

Clichés are no more evident than in commentary on current events, whether headlines, reviews, or publicity. Politicians are perhaps the proudest conveyors of clichés and platitudes. According to *Time* magazine, "Our most cliché-ridden presidents were also our greater ones . . . What former presidents seemed to understand was that often repeated, hackneyed sentiments—if spoken by someone who really felt them—were, above everything, what Americans wanted to hear." Like presidents, when you are holding forth, by using clichés, proverbs, and platitudes, your opinions will garner respect—and likely be repeated by others.

Art

You can't judge a book by its cover.

———•◦•———

A picture is worth a thousand words.

———•◦•———

The worst singers sing the loudest.

———•◦•———

Practice not your art and
it will soon depart.

———•◦•———

A poet is born, not made.

———•◦•———

Art has no enemy but ignorance.

———•◦•———

He that paints a flower does
not give it perfume.

———•◦•———

It is easier to criticize art than create it.

———•◦•———

He who sings drives away sorrow.

The pen is mightier than the sword.

———•·•———

A fine painter chooses his
brushes carefully.

———•·•———

Even the best writer has to erase.

———•·•———

Music soothes the savage beast.

———•·•———

The devil makes the best music.

———•·•———

Art is long and life is short.

———•·•———

There's nothing new under the sun.

———•·•———

The poor writer blames the pen.

———•·•———

Art imitates life.

———•·•———

All the world's a stage.

You can't fill your belly
painting pictures of bread.

A book is like a garden
carried in the pocket.

We're fools whether we dance or
not so we might as well dance.

Everyone will have their
fifteen minutes of fame.

Any publicity is good publicity.

Food and Drink

You are what you eat.

Eat to live, not live to eat.

Beer before liquor, never sicker;
liquor before beer, you're in the clear.

He that is unkind to his own
will not be kind to others.

A community is as those who rule it.

Become not a priest in your hometown,
nor marry far away from it.

Close neighbors are better
than distant relatives.

United we stand, divided we fall.

Live together or die alone.

CULTURE

When all the world's a stage

CULTURAL INTERESTS ALLOW US
to connect and bond, providing us
with endless fodder for dinner-party
conversation and chats with strang-
ers. When it comes to our hobbies
and habits, platitudes are cultural
currency, comprising a common
platform from which to relate
and dissect the makeup of civiliza-
tion itself.

Lost in Translation

When it comes to international relations, language matters; a misinterpreted idiomatic phrase could spark global conflict. Fortunately, the powers that be recognize this. During the Cold War, President Richard Nixon studied up on Russian maxims to facilitate negotiation, and today the United Nations offers the language course Arabic Culture Through Proverbs "to investigate the patterns of life, culture, politics, ethics, society, religion, and history."

The poet W. H. Auden said, "Some books are undeservedly forgotten; none are undeservedly remembered." The Canadian *National Post* noted, "Possibly that rule applies also to words, terms, phrases, even comparisons to icebergs. Longevity confirms their value." Art, ideas, performances, and gastronomy last in our collective memories just as

There is truth in wine.

———•◆•———

Choose your company before
you choose your drink.

———•◆•———

Better to burst the belly
than spoil good food.

———•◆•———

The way to a man's heart is
through his stomach.

Tip: Ignorance Is Bliss

In the 1979 film *Being There*, Peter Sellers
stars as a simple-minded gardener whose
knowledge of the world comes entirely
from television. He speaks in enigmatic
platitudes—"There are spring and summer,
but there are also fall and winter"—that
are deemed brilliant by influential people,
including the president. If you wish others
to think you wise, merely express yourself in
clichés—their projection will do the rest.

Hunger is the best sauce.

———•———

The eye is bigger than the belly.

———•———

The nearer the cow, the better the cheese.

———•———

A clean pig makes lean bacon.

———•———

Pork has many different
flavors, all of them good.

———•———

The proof of the pudding is in the eating.

———•———

Cheap meat never makes a good soup.

———•———

No man will feed on herbs
when meat is to be had.

———•———

A meal without wine is like
a day without sunshine.

He who eats alone chokes alone.

———•◦•———

Man cannot live by bread alone.

———•◦•———

More people are drowned in
the glass than the sea.

———•◦•———

No dish pleases all palates alike.

———•◦•———

First come, first served.

———•◦•———

Eat, drink, and be merry, for
tomorrow we die.

———•◦•———

There are starving children in Africa.

Sports

There's no "I" in team.

———•◦•———

Float like a butterfly, sting like a bee.

Play Ball

Sportscasters are notorious for inventing clever—and not so clever—turns of phrase. Harry Caray, the beloved Chicago Cubs announcer, popularized "holy cow," while Chick Hearn, voice of the Los Angeles Lakers, introduced "slam dunk" and "air ball." Football commentator John Madden is known for his "Maddenisms," which often state the obvious, such as this informative chestnut: "You can't win the game if you don't score any points."

Victory has a hundred fathers
but defeat is an orphan.

Never tell a foe that your foot hurts.

Give it 110 percent.

Before you can score, you
must have a goal.

You can't measure the
heart of a champion.

———•———

A man surprised is half beaten.

———•———

Sweat makes good mortar.

———•———

You can't win 'em all.

———•———

It's a whole new ball game.

———•———

The strong man's sport
is the sickly man's death.

———•———

The thrill of victory,
the agony of defeat.

———•———

All are not hunters who blow the horn.

———•———

To the winner go the spoils.

You win some, you lose some.

———•———

The best defense is a good offense.

———•———

Keep your eye on the ball.

———•———

A defeated wrestler is not
tired of wrestling.

———•———

A cock can't ride horseback
although he has spurs.

———•———

It's not whether you win or lose,
it's how you play the game.

———•———

No guts, no glory.

———•———

Winning isn't everything.

———•———

Win one for the Gipper.

History

All roads lead to Rome.

Might makes right.

The courts of kings are full
of men, empty of friends.

Truth is the first casualty of war.

An ambassador bears no blame.

When elephants fight,
it is the grass that suffers.

He that cannot obey
cannot command.

The greatest empire may be lost
by the misrule of its governors.

Politics makes strange bedfellows.

I came, I saw, I conquered.

Lofty towers fall with a heavier crash.

It is easy to rule over the good.

An army of sheep led by a lion would
defeat an army of lions led by a sheep.

Those who cannot remember the
past are condemned to repeat it.

Absolute power corrupts absolutely.

History is written by the winners.

The more things change, the
more they stay the same.

Nothing is certain except the past.

I am not a crook.

Let them eat cake.

Rock the vote.

Yes we can.

"Time for Change"

Stating that then–presidential hopeful Barack Obama "has more clichés in his vocabulary than you can shake a stick at," Irish bookmaking agency Paddy Power took bets on which phrases Obama would use when accepting the Democratic nomination in 2008. The favorite, with six-to-one odds, was "I'm fired up." At five hundred-to-one, the offensive "Always bet on black" was a far riskier wager. Unfortunately for bettors, Obama said neither.

LIFE AND DEATH

When what goes around comes around

CLICHÉS FOLLOW US FROM CRADLE
to grave. Whether we are indulg-
ing in chitchat, monitoring our
well-being, or facing the end of the
road, in matters great and small
platitudes support our endeavors.
Outlooks on life are either glass
half-full or half-empty, rose-colored
glasses or gloom and doom, and
there are well-trodden expressions
to support both.

Rumor Mill

During the Civil War, battle news was dispatched via what came to be known as the "grapevine telegraph" based on the resemblance between the tree-hanging wires and the plant. The technology was so notoriously unreliable that the term became synonymous with the course a rumor takes. In 1968, Marvin Gaye spread the phrase—without misunderstanding—far and wide with the chart-topping song "I Heard It Through the Grapevine."

The purity of clichés distills life's big themes, making them manageable and relatable. While we have a tendency to disparage gossip, there's no doubt that it's always existed and will never cease. Indeed, tattle is most likely human nature, that overarching generator of proverbs and platitudes. People who live in glass houses may not want to throw stones, but how many of us live in glass houses? When talking about others, by employing previously said phrases, you will appear less culpable of ill spirit.

Speaking to matters of health and death requires the most discretion and skill, but with clichés, you'll always be armed with the appropriate wisdom. Tried-and-true expressions are even fitting for your final words. The tombstones of cartoon legend Mel Blanc and talk-show host Merv Griffin read, respectively, "That's all folks" and "I will *not* be right back after this message." After death, you'll want to leave a lasting impression, so plan ahead—choose a cliché from these pages and don't forget to let your family know of your posthumous desire.

Gossip

Where there's smoke, there's fire.

———•—•———

Throw enough dirt and some will stick.

———•—•———

Loose lips sink ships.

———•—•———

Every ass loves to hear himself bray.

———•—•———

Scandal is like an egg:
when it hatches, it has wings.

———•—•———

People who live in glass houses
shouldn't throw stones.

———•—•———

Sticks and stones may break
my bones, but words will never hurt me.

———•—•———

Three may keep a secret,
if two of them are dead.

Don't air your dirty laundry in public.

Curses, like chickens, come
home to roost.

There are two sides to every story.

The shallower the brook
the more it babbles.

The cat's out of the bag.

If you don't have anything nice to
say then don't say anything at all.

Discretion is the better part of valor.

Ask me no questions and
I'll tell you no lies.

Bad news travels fast.

Least said, soonest mended.

Let sleeping dogs lie.

Health

An apple a day keeps the doctor away.

Early to bed and early to rise makes
a man healthy, wealthy, and wise.

Feed a cold and starve a fever.

Laughter is the best medicine.

Health is better than wealth.

Even the leper thinks ill of the syphilitic.

An ounce of prevention is
worth a pound of cure.

Garlic is as good as ten mothers.

———◆◆◆———

The cure is worse than the disease.

———◆◆◆———

Let nature take its course.

———◆◆◆———

Health is not valued 'til sickness comes.

———◆◆◆———

What cannot be cured must be endured.

Talk Is...

Clichés, song lyrics, and expletives are
considered automatic (vs. creative) forms
of speech. Patients suffering from impaired
creative speech due to brain damage retain
these reflexive speech functions because
they originate from a different part of the
brain. Proverb-completion exercises (such as
"Misery loves _____") help in diagnosing certain types of aphasia, determining the severity
of the condition and the course of treatment.

God cures and the physician
takes the fee.

Every patient is a doctor after his cure.

There's no such thing as an
atheist in a foxhole.

Death

Death waits for no one.

Ashes to ashes, dust to dust.

A beautiful funeral
doesn't guarantee heaven.

Never speak ill of the dead.

Rooster today,
feather duster tomorrow.

Death always comes too early or too late.

———•———

Dying is as natural as living.

———•———

All steps end in the grave.

———•———

The first breath is
the beginning of death.

———•———

You only live once.

———•———

Never murder a man who is
about to commit suicide.

———•———

We are no more than candles
blowing in the wind.

———•———

A good death honors a long life.

———•———

It takes four living men to carry
one dead man out of a house.

Tip: There Are No Words

Death is far too overwhelming, complicated, and traumatic to create an original response, so it's best not to try. When speaking to the grief-stricken, skillfully implemented clichés are an absolute necessity, the tried-and-true solace of the familiar. Combined with offers of assistance ("What can I do?"), traditional condolences are safe, warm, and fuzzy, which makes it easier to avoid saying the wrong thing—at the very worst time.

Six feet of earth make all men equal.

———

Regret magnifies the loss.

———

Only the good die young.

———

Nothing is certain but death and taxes.

———

Life's a bitch and then you die.

Optimism

Every cloud has a silver lining.

———•———

An elephant is not burdened by its tusks.

———•———

When life hands you lemons,
make lemonade.

———•———

Life is a bowl of cherries.

———•———

Don't worry, be happy.

———•———

Something's better than nothing.

———•———

It's not the end of the world.

———•———

I'm okay, you're okay.

———•———

Even a blind pig finds
an acorn now and then.

The man who tickles himself
can laugh when he chooses.

———•———

A rising tide lifts all boats.

———•———

Better to light one candle than
to curse the darkness.

———•———

It's always darkest before the dawn.

———•———

Carpe diem.

———•———

Never say never.

———•———

Hope springs eternal.

———•———

Whatever doesn't kill you
makes you stronger.

———•———

A journey of a thousand miles
begins with the first step.

Today is the first day
of the rest of your life.

———————

Tomorrow is another day.

Pessimism

If you want peace,
you must prepare for war.

———————

The tongue always returns
to the sore tooth.

———————

Nothing in life is free.

———————

Experience is the comb that nature
gives us when we are bald.

———————

Trust in God, but tie your camel.

———————

If wishes were horses,
beggars would ride.

Give a man rope enough
and he will hang himself.

The road to hell is paved
with good intentions.

What can you expect
from a pig but a grunt?

Anything that can go
wrong will go wrong.

Nice guys finish last.

Be careful what you wish for—
you might get it.

You can't make a silk purse
out of a sow's ear.

If it sounds too good to be true,
then it probably is.

Chicken merry, hawk is near.

One lark does not make it spring.

No good deed goes unpunished.

It's a dog-eat-dog world.

Shit happens.

Half-Full or Half-Empty?

One of the many legacies of A. A. Milne's
Winnie-the-Pooh is the division of humankind
into two clichéd sorts: Tiggers or Eeyores.
Tiggers, named after the frisky tiger charac-
ter, are full of energy and optimism, while
Eeyores, consistent with the sad-eyed donkey,
are gloomy pessimists. The message, of
course, is that it takes all kinds. In the words
of Eeyore, "We can't all, and some of us don't.
That's all there is to it."